ACROSS THE PLAINS IN 1844

CATHERINE SAGER

WITH A BONUS BOOK FROM
ELIZA SPALDING

ACROSS THE PLAINS IN 1844

CATHERINE SAGER

INTRODUCTION

Catherine Sager's story is among the most gripping firsthand accounts of life in the American West ever written. This enhanced version of her original manuscript adds explanatory notes, photos, maps, drawings, and 3d visualizations. Sager's story is a fascinating read all by itself—this bonus material adds a layer of context to bring the story alive even more.

Catherine Sager faced almost unimaginable hardship: both her parents died on the journey west on the Oregon Trail; a few years later her adoptive parents were murdered. She was even kidnapped and held for ransom. Yet Catherine was a survivor, and she lived a long life in Oregon. Her accounts of life on the Oregon Trail and the tragedy at Waiilatpu remain important historical documents. At the same time, she is an excellent writer who knows how to engage the reader.

Michael Trinklein, editor

CHAPTER
ONE
ON THE PLAINS IN 1844

My father was one of the restless ones who are not content to remain in one place long at a time. Late in the fall of 1838 we emigrated from Ohio to Missouri. Our first halting place was on Green River, but the next year we took a farm in Platte County. He engaged in farming and black-smithing, and had a wide reputation for ingenuity. Anything they needed, made or mended, sought his shop. In 1843, Dr. Whitman came to Missouri.

The healthful climate induced my mother to favor moving to Oregon. Immigration was the theme all winter, and we decided to start for Oregon. Late in 1843 father sold his property and moved near St. Joseph, and in April, 1844, we started across the plains. The first encampments were a great pleasure to us children. We were five girls and two boys, ranging from the girl baby to be born on the way to the oldest boy, hardly old enough to be any help.

Catherine does not spell it out, but Dr. Marcus Whitman (pictured here) played a major role in encouraging the Sager family to go to Oregon. Whitman was one of the first settlers to go west on the Oregon Trail, setting up a Presbyterian mission near what is now Walla Walla in 1836. At this point in Catherine's story, he has returned to Missouri to encourage others to make the journey.

STARTING ON THE PLAINS

We waited several days at the Missouri River. Many friends came that far to see the emigrants start on their long journey, and there was much sadness at the parting, and a sorrowful company crossed the

Missouri that bright spring morning.

The Missouri River crossing was a bottleneck on the Oregon Trail; like a modern traffic jam.

The motion of the wagon made us all sick, and it was weeks before we got used to the seasick motion. Rain came down and required us to tie down the wagon covers, and so increased our sickness by confining the air we breathed.

Our cattle recrossed in the night and went back to their winter quarters. This caused delay in recovering them and a weary, forced march to rejoin the train. This was divided into companies, and we were in that commanded by William Shaw. Soon after starting Indians raided our camp one night and drove off a number of cattle. They were pursued, but never recovered.

Soon everything went smooth and our train made steady headway. The weather was fine and we enjoyed the journey pleasantly. There were several musical instruments among the emigrants, and these sounded clearly on the evening air when camp was made and merry talk and laughter resounded from almost every camp-fire.

INCIDENTS OF TRAVEL

We had one wagon, two steady yoke of old cattle, and several of young and not well-broken ones. Father was no ox driver, and had trouble with these until one day he called on Captain Shaw for assistance. It was furnished by the good captain pelting the refractory steers with stones until they were glad to come to terms.

NOTES

EDITOR'S NOTE: Like the majority of overland pioneers, the Sagers pulled their wagons with oxen, not horses. Oxen were slow and plodding, but they could graze more effectively than horses. While it's easy to assume that all the overland pioneers were experts with animals, this was far from the truth. Catherine readily admits her father needed help learning how to manage the oxen.

Reaching the buffalo country, our father would get some one to drive his team and start on the hunt, for he was enthusiastic in his love of such sport. He not only killed the great bison, but often brought home on his shoulder the timid antelope that had fallen at his unerring aim, and that are not often shot by ordinary marksmen.

At this point, bison were plentiful. In later years, indiscriminate hunting would bring the bison to near-extinction.

Soon after crossing South Platte the unwieldy oxen ran on a bank and overturned the wagon, greatly injuring our mother. She lay long insensible in the tent put up for the occasion.

August 1st we nooned in a beautiful grove on the north side of the Platte. We had by this time got used to climbing in and out of the wagon when in motion. When performing this feat that afternoon my dress caught on an axle helve and I was thrown under the wagon wheel, which passed over and badly crushed my limb before father could stop the team. He picked me up and saw the extent of the injury when the injured limb hung dangling in the air.

NOTES

EDITOR'S NOTE: Catherine seems quite matter-of-fact about what appears to be a very significant injury—a broken leg "dangling" after she was run over by the wagon. Sadly, these injuries were not uncommon on the Oregon Trail—and many children were killed when they were run over by the heavy wagons.

THE FATHER DYING ON THE PLAINS

In a broken voice he exclaimed: "My dear child, your leg is broken all to pieces!" The news soon spread along the train and a halt was called. A surgeon was found and the limb set; then we pushed on the same night to Laramie, where we arrived soon after dark. This accident confined me to the wagon for the remainder of the long journey.

After Laramie we entered the great American

desert, which was hard on the teams. Sickness became common. Father and the boys were all sick, and we were dependent for a driver on the Dutch doctor who set my leg. He offered his services and was employed, but though an excellent surgeon, he knew little about driving oxen. Some of them often had to rise from their sick beds to wade streams and get the oxen safely across. One day four buffalo ran between our wagon and the one behind. Though feeble, father seized his gun and gave chase to them. This imprudent act prostrated him again, and it soon became apparent that his days were numbered. He was fully conscious of the fact, but could not be reconciled to the thought of leaving his large and helpless family in such precarious circumstances. The evening before his death we crossed Green River and camped on the bank. Looking where I lay helpless, he said: "Poor child! What will become of you?" Captain Shaw found him weeping bitterly. He said his last hour had come, and his heart was filled with anguish for his family. His wife was ill, the children small, and one likely to be a cripple. They had no relatives near, and a long journey lay before them. In piteous tones he begged the Captain to take charge of them and see them through. This he stoutly promised. Father was buried the next day on the banks of Green River. His coffin was made of two troughs dug out of the body of a tree, but next year emigrants found his bleaching bones, as the Indians had disinterred the remains.

N O T E S

EDITOR'S NOTE: We don't know exactly what disease killed Catherine's father. The most common illness on the Oregon Trail—cholera—almost always took its victims quickly, within a day or two. Catherine implies her father gradually got worse over time, leading some to conclude he had scurvy, a vitamin deficiency. If it was scurvy, tomatoes, potatoes, or even sour kraut would have saved him. But those foods were unavailable on the trail. Most overland pioneers ate a steady diet of pan-cooked bread and salted bacon, foods that would keep on a long journey.

We hired a young man to drive, as mother was afraid to trust the doctor, but the kindhearted German would not leave her, and declared his intention to see her safe in the Willamette. At Fort Bridger the stream was full of fish, and we made nets of wagon sheets to catch them.

This accurate re-creation of Ft. Bridger shows the fort as Catherine would have seen it.

That evening the new driver told mother he would hunt for game if she would let him use the gun. He took it, and we never saw him again. He made for the train in advance, where he had a sweetheart. We found the gun waiting our arrival at Whitman's. Then we got along as best we could with the doctor's help.

Mother planned to get to Whitman's and winter there, but she was rapidly failing under her sorrows. The nights and mornings were very cold, and she took cold from the exposure unavoidably. With camp fever and a sore mouth, she fought bravely against fate for the sake of her children, but she was taken delirious soon after reaching Fort Bridger, and was bed-fast. Traveling in this condition over a road clouded with dust, she suffered intensely. She talked of her husband, addressing him as though present, beseeching him in piteous tones to relieve her sufferings, until at last she became unconscious. Her babe was cared for by the women of the train. Those kind-hearted women would also come in at night and wash the dust from the mother's face and otherwise make her comfortable. We traveled a rough road the day she died, and she moaned fearfully all the time. At night one of the women came in as usual, but she made no reply to questions, so she thought her asleep, and washed her face, then took her hand and discovered the pulse was nearly gone. She lived but a few moments, and her last words were, "Oh, Henry! If you only knew how we have suffered." The tent was set up, the corpse laid out, and next morning we took the last look at our mother's face. The grave was near the road; willow brush was laid in the bottom and covered the body, the earth filled in — then the train moved on.

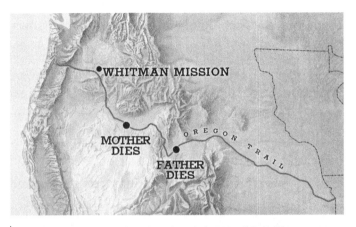

Catherine Sager's father was buried near the Green River in what is now southwest Wyoming. Her mother was buried near what is now Twin Falls, Idaho. The children were then adopted by Narcissa and Marcus Whitman at the Whitman Mission.

Her name was cut on a headboard, and that was all that could be done. So in twenty-six days we became orphans. Seven children of us, the oldest fourteen and the youngest a babe. A few days before her death, finding herself in possession of her faculties and fully aware of the coming end, she had taken an affectionate farewell of her children and charged the doctor to take care of us. She made the same request of Captain Shaw. The baby was taken by a woman in the train, and all were literally adopted by the company. No one there but was ready to do us any possible favor. This was especially true of Captain Shaw and his wife. Their kindness will ever be cherished in grateful remembrance by us all. Our parents could not have been more solicitous or careful. When our flour gave out they gave us bread as long as they had any, actually dividing their last loaf. To this day Uncle Billy and Aunt Sally, as we call them, regard us with the affection of parents. Blessings on his hoary head!

At Snake River they lay by to make our wagon into a cart, as our team was wearing out. Into this was loaded what was necessary. Some things were sold and some left on the plains. The last of September we arrived at Grande Ronde, where one of my sister's clothes caught fire, and she would have burned to death only that the German doctor, at the cost of burning his hands, saved her. One night the captain heard a child crying, and found my little sister had got out of the wagon and was perishing in the freezing air, for the nights were very cold. We had been out of flour and living on meat alone, so a few were sent in advance to get supplies from Dr. Whitman and return to us. Having so light a load we could travel faster than the other teams, and went on with Captain Shaw and the advance. Through the Blue Mountains cattle were giving out and left lying in the road. We made but a few miles a day. We were in the country of "Dr. Whitman's Indians," as they called themselves. They were returning from buffalo hunting and frequented our camps. They were loud in praise of the missionaries and anxious to assist us. Often they would drive up some beast that had been left behind as given out and return it to its owner.

N O T E S

EDITOR'S NOTE: In the Oregon Trail's early years, stories of Native American helpfulness were common— as Catherine Sager notes. Often the tribes helped round up loose cattle or assisted in river crossings. Later, after a series of U.S. military attacks on the Native Americans, cordial relations dissipated.

One day when we were making a fire of wet wood Francis thought to help the matter by holding his powder-horn over a small blaze. Of course the powder-horn exploded, and the wonder was he was left alive. He ran to a creek near by and bathed his hands and face, and came back destitute of winkers and eyebrows, and his face was blackened beyond recognition. Such were the incidents and dangerous and humorous features of the journey.

We reached Umatilla October 15th, and lay by while Captain Shaw went on to Whitman's station to see if the doctor would take care of us, if only until he could become located in the Willamette. We purchased of the Indians the first potatoes we had eaten since we started on our long and sad journey. October 17th we started for our destination, leaving the baby very sick, with doubts of its recovery. Mrs. Shaw took an affectionate leave of us all, and stood looking after us as long as we were in sight. Speaking of it in later years, she said she never saw a more pitiful sight than that cartful of orphans going to find a home among strangers.

We reached the station in the forenoon. For weeks this place had been a subject for our talk by day and formed our dreams at night. We expected to see log houses, occupied by Indians and such people as we had seen about the forts. Instead we saw a large white house surrounded with palisades. A short distance from the doctor's dwelling was another large adobe house, built by Mr. Gray, but now used by immigrants in the winter, and for a granary in the summer. It was situated near the mill pond, and the grist mill was not far from it.

Between the two houses were the blacksmith shop and the corral, enclosed with slabs set up endways. The garden lay between the mill and the house, and a large field was on the opposite side. A good-sized ditch passed in front of the house, connecting with the mill pond, intersecting other ditches all around the farm, for the purpose of irrigating the land.

Here is the layout of the Whitman Mission. It was also known as "Waiilatpu"

We drove up and halted near this ditch. Captain Shaw was in the house conversing with Mrs. Whitman. Glancing through the window, he saw us, and turning to her said: "Your children have come; will you go out and see them?" He then came out and told the boys to "Help the girls out and get their bonnets." Alas! it was easy to talk of bonnets, but not to find them! But one or two were finally discovered by the time Mrs. Whitman had come out. Here was a scene for an artist to describe! Foremost stood the little cart, with the tired oxen that had been unyoked lying near it. Sitting in the front end of the cart was John, weeping bitterly; on the opposite side stood Francis, his arms on the wheel and his head resting on his arms, sobbing aloud; on the near side the little girls were huddled together, bareheaded and barefooted, looking at the boys and then at the house, dreading we knew not what. By the oxen stood the good German doctor, with his whip in his hand, regarding the scene with suppressed emotion.

Thus Mrs. Whitman found us. She was a large, well-formed woman, fair complexioned, with beautiful auburn hair, nose rather large, and large gray eyes. She had on a dark calico dress and gingham sunbonnet. We thought as we shyly looked at her that she was the prettiest woman we had ever seen.

| *Narcissa Whitman, who adopted the Sager children.*

She spoke kindly to us as she came up, but like frightened things we ran behind the cart, peeping shyly around at her. She then addressed the boys, asking why they wept, adding: "Poor boys. no wonder you weep!" She then began to arrange things as we threw them out, at the same time conversing with an Indian woman sitting on the ground near by. A little girl about seven years old soon came and stood regarding us with a timid look. This was little Helen Mar Meed, and though a half-breed, she looked very pretty to us in her green dress and white apron and neat sunbonnet.

Having arranged everything in compact form Mrs. Whitman directed the doctor and the boys where to carry them, and told Helen to show the little girls the way to the house. Seeing my lameness, she kindly took me by the hand and my little sister by the other hand, and thus led us in. As we reached the steps, Captain Shaw asked if she had children of her own. Pointing to a grave at the foot of the hill not far off, she said: "All the child I ever had sleeps yonder." She added that it was a great pleasure to her that she could see the grave from the door. The doctor and boys having deposited the things as directed, went over to the mansion. As we entered the house we saw a girl about nine years old washing dishes. Mrs. Whitman spoke cheerfully to her and said: "Well, Mary Ann, how do you think you will like all these sisters?" Seated in her arm-chair, she placed the youngest on her lap, and calling us round her, asked our names about our parents, and the baby, often exclaiming as we told our artless story, "Poor children!"

Dr. Whitman came in from the mill and stood in the door, looking as though surprised at the large addition so suddenly made to the family. We were a sight calculated to excite surprise, dirty and sunburned until we looked more like Indians than white children. Added to this, John had cropped our hair so that it hung in uneven locks and added to our uncouth appearance. Seeing her husband standing there, Mrs. Whitman said, with a laugh: "Come in, doctor, and see your children." He sat down and tried to take little Louisa in his arms, but she ran screaming to me, much to the discomfiture of the doctor and amusement of his wife. She then related to him what we had told her in reference to the baby, and expressed her fears lest it should die, saying it was the baby she wanted most of all.

Our mother had asked that we might not be separated, so Captain Shaw now urged the doctor to take charge of us all. He feared the Board might object, as he was sent as a missionary to the Indians. The captain argued that a missionary's duty was to do good, and we certainly were objects worthy of missionary charity. He was finally persuaded to keep us all until spring. His wife did not readily consent, but he told her he wanted boys as well as the girls. Finding the boys willing to stay, he made a written agreement with Captain Shaw that he would take charge of them. Before Captain Show reached the valley, Dr. Whitman overtook him and told him he was pleased with the children and he need give himself no further care concerning them. The baby was brought over in few days. It was very sick, but under Mrs. Whitman's judicious care was soon restored to health.

Our faithful friend, the German doctor, left us at last, safe in the motherly care of Mrs. Whitman. Well had he kept his promise to our dying mother.

For a week or two the house at Waiilatpu was full of company. Having no help, Mrs. Whitman was too much engaged in household affairs to pay any attention to us. Very lonely did that large house seem to me during that time. Being a cripple, I was not able to join the other children in their pastimes, and they were too busy enjoying themselves to attend to me. Seated by the cradle, I plied my needle at simple sewing. I saw my brothers only at meal-time. Mrs. Whitman came occasionally to bring the baby her milk. I thought I could never be happy where everything was so strange, and shed many tears in solitude. I became so timid as to cry if addressed by the doctor or any one.

School commenced soon after our arrival, and most of the children In course of time the company left the home; help was hired to do the housework, and Mrs. Whitman, having more time to herself, paid more to us.

attended.

Gathering us around her in the evening, she amused us with anecdotes, distributing pieces of calico and showing us how to make patchwork and rag dolls, conversing with us in a kind and familiar way. On one of these occasions she gave each of us a string of beads

SCHOOL

School was held in the back part of the main building at the Whitman Mission.

to wear, with the understanding that anyone who had to be reproved for doing wrong must return the beads to her. We had been long without restraint, so that we had become quite unruly and difficult to manage. They were strict disciplinarians, and held the reins with steady hands. Any deviation from the rules met with instant and severe chastisement. Every effort to merit their approval was rewarded with smiles. While we were held under strict subjection, every effort was made to render us comfortable and happy and to win our love and confidence. Mrs. Whitman was particularly adapted to raising chil-

dren, having the art of uniting instruction and pleasure. She was a fine singer. I have never known
anyone who excelled her in this respect. She soon
commenced teaching us vocal music. Refined and
accomplished herself, she exercised over our rude
natures that influence that refines and beautifies a
home. We soon formed a warm attachment for her,
and fell into the practice of calling her and Dr.
Whitman mother and father, as the other children
did, and continued it while they lived. They were
careful to have us remember our parents, and would
speak of them with affection and respect. When
necessary to administer punishment, she would set
our fault before us and her own responsibility, and
show that all was done for our own good, and would
ask what we thought our parents would wish her
to do.

Dr. Whitman's family, before we came, consisted
of himself and wife, Perrin P. Whitman, his nephew,
who came out with him in 1843, when fourteen
years old; Mary Ann Bridger, nine years old; Helen
Mar Meek, seven years old, who had been raised
from infancy by Mrs. Whitman, and David M.
Cortez, seven years old. This boy's father was a
Spaniard, his mother a Walla Walla Indian. Becoming
tired of the infant, she cast it into a hole to perish.
His grandmother rescued him and took him to Mrs.

Whitman, naked, except a small piece of skin tied over his shoulders.

EDITOR'S NOTE: The Whitmans were the first family to travel to Oregon Country by covered wagon—making the trek in 1836 along with Henry and Eliza Spalding, and a few others. (Catherine spells it "Spaulding" but the more common spelling is "Spalding.") The Whitmans and Spaldings came as missionaries to the native people, and were the only white settlers in the region for many years. So when the Sager children were orphaned in 1843, the Whitmans were the logical choice to take them in.

We were in the schoolroom from Monday morning until Saturday noon. The afternoon was a holiday. If the weather was pleasant, the preparations for the Sabbath being completed, Mrs. Whitman took us out for a ramble over the hills. In inclement weather we were provided amusement in the house; the doctor believed in young folks having plenty of exercise. The Sabbath was always strictly observed, yet made so pleasant that we hailed its dawn with delight. Every preparation was made the day before, and perfect stillness pervaded the house Sabbath morning. In the winter season a Bible class met on Saturday night. All the family attended, and no effort was spared to make it interesting. A subject was given us to prove from the Bible, and Mrs. Whitman saw that each child had a proof to bring in. They were commented on, a chapter was read, each one reading a verse and giving their thoughts on it. These exercises closed by singing some Bible hymn. Sabbath morning we were reminded of the day and all kept still. Each sat with a book, and those too small to read were handed pictures. After breakfast we prepared for Sunday school, that met at 11 o'clock, while the doctor held his service with the natives. Each got seven verses, one being learned every morning during the week. This was an interesting hour spent together, especially when the doctor could spend some moments with us. At 3 P.M. we met for the regular afternoon service, when Dr. Whitman read a sermon. He was not a preacher, but a physician. We had to find the text after the service was over and repeat it to him. The evening was spent in reading, reciting the commandments, etc.

N O T E S

EDITOR'S NOTE: While Catherine is quite correct in stating that Marcus Whitman was not a preacher, he had wanted to become one. But without the funds for a minister's training, he settled on becoming a doctor—which was a shorter course of study at that time. Even though Whitman was not formally trained as a minister, both he and Narcissa were deeply religious, and came west out of a desire to serve God by reaching out to the native peoples of the American west.

One evening in the week Mrs. Whitman would collect the young around her, holding a prayer meeting with them and conversing on religious subjects. The first Monday night in each month a meeting was held in behalf of missions, and Monday after New Year's was observed as a fast day. The housework was hired done in winter, so the children could follow their studies without hindrance; Mrs. Whitman and the girls did the work in the summer. Each of us had her allotted task and was expected to promptly do her duty. At 11 we bathed in the river; dinner was served at 12. When the work was done we all sat in a large room at our sewing, save one of us, who read aloud to the rest. Supper was at 5 o'clock, and after that was over time until retiring for the night was devoted to recreation. In the spring the evenings were spent in the garden putting in seeds; otherwise we did as we pleased. Sometimes the boys would bring horses for us to ride; at times we would go with the doctor to visit the lodges, where Indians were sick. Mrs. Whitman was always with us in all these occupations, adding to our enjoyment. She was very fond of flowers, and we assisted in taking care of her flower garden each season. Our time flowed on in one uninterrupted stream of pleasure; we were kept constantly gaining knowledge, and from morning until night our adopted parents labored to promote our happiness. The family was larger in the winter. From twenty to twenty-five, including children, sat around the table at meals. Besides the adopted children, there were others who came to attend the mission school. Summers the doctor was gone most of the time, so there was only Mrs. Whitman and the children. Mr. Spaulding's daughter attended school with us. She came on horseback, in charge of an Indian woman, 120 miles.

The manner of living was simple. In winter we had beef, and in summer mutton and fish. Pork seldom came on the table. Dr. Whitman ignored fine flour, and wheat flour and corn meal were used unbolted. Tea and coffee came to the table only on rare occasions. This was a matter of economy as delicacies were not easy to get in the country at that time. There was an abundance of wild fruit to be purchased of the natives; a good garden supplied plenty of vegetables. Cake and pastry only were seen on holidays. Milk, butter and cheese were in full supply, and thus you have our mode of living at Waiilatpu.

Catherine mentions "Mr. Spaulding's daughter" who attended school with the Sagers. This would have been Eliza Spaulding, whose parents set up a mission similar to the Whitman's —about 120 miles east. Based on an existing photo, above is an artist's rendering of what Eliza looked like at about 8-years-old. Young Eliza was one of the few white people in the region who could speak the native language. This became very important later on.

Some may ask how the washing for so large a family was managed. As early as 4 o'clock all hands were mustered for work in the kitchen, Mrs. Whitman at the head. Tubs and barrels were put in use, and all the implements needed were at hand. The boys, with long aprons tied around them, brought the water and did the pounding, while the women rubbed the clothes. Jokes were current and all were in good humor. By school time (9 o'clock) the clothes were on the line. It fell to the lot of myself and brother to get breakfast on wash days.

Owing to the location and the evaporation in the spring of alkali ponds near by, Waiilatpu was not healthy. The mill pond was near by, and we were more or less troubled with chills and fever in warm weather. I was very subject to it, and suffered every summer of my stay there, being often unable to labor. As the eldest daughter, I had supervision of the other girls, and from being confined to the house so much I became the constant companion of Mrs. Whitman. An attachment near to that of mother and daughter existed between us from this constant association. To me she told all her plans for the pleasure or improvement of the children, as well as her fears and troubles concerning them. When the doctor was long absent I sat with her and read or conversed, and was her bedfellow. She said often she could not get along without me.

The spring after we arrived brother Francis resolved to run away to the lower country with those who had wintered there. His reason was he disliked the strict discipline maintained. The doctor was away, and when Francis started to go Mrs. Whitman urged him pleasantly to stay, but he went on the run, mounted his horse, and was off before the wagons moved which he was to accompany. She had not succeeded in winning the boy's confidence and affection, and Francis was stubborn.

Efforts were made to overtake him and get him to come back, but they were unavailing. He went to the Willamette and remained there.

On his return Dr. Whitman talked with John and found he was willing to remain. He then made a proposal to aid the boys to get a start in cattle and horses, so that they would be acquiring property. This was made known to Francis by a letter, and a horse sent for him, so that in the fall we had the pleasure of again becoming a united family.

In the spring of 1845 the Cayuses were embroiled in war with the Snakes. A Cayuse family named Prince was going to the buffalo country to hunt, and on the way camped on a small stream in the Snake region, opposite a camp of Snake Indians. One morning Prince with his servant rode over to see the other camp. His horse stood all day tied at the Snake lodge, but the mother did not go to learn about him, because her daughter said it would be foolish. Toward night the horse disappeared, and during the night the Snake camp also disappeared. Going over there, the mother and daughter found the dead bodies of servant and master. War resulted, in which many Cayuses lost their lives, including some of their chiefs. We saw them come home from their war raids, and heard and saw them singing war songs, dancing their war dances, and then they would change to a funeral dirge for their dead warriors. After a successful raid they would spend days in celebrating their victory and reciting the prowess of their own warriors. The beating of drums and their war-whoops and songs filled the air with savage sounds. The monotonous tones of the Indian flute mellowed the horrors of the din a little.

NOTES

EDITOR'S NOTE: Catherine references the "Snake" Indians—a term that pioneers used to refer to the Northern Paiute, Bannock, or Shoshone peoples. The Cayuse were the people the Whitmans originally traveled west to serve.

One Sunday morning in the autumn of 1845 two men arrived at the station. One of them, Andrew Rodgers, was a young man of about twenty-five, tall and slender, sandy hair and sallow look that betokened ill-health. He sang hymns and played the violin, so the "Seceders," to which church he belonged, turned him out. His gentlemanly appearance and intelligence won the admiration of Dr. and Mrs. Whitman. He came to procure room and care for a friend who was ill with consumption. He succeeded in this and was also engaged to teach school the ensuing winter. Going to Umatilla, he soon returned with his friend, Joseph Finly, who took board with the family of Mr. Osborne, his relative. He had made the journey to Oregon hoping for improved health. For awhile he improved and seemed stronger. Dr. and Mrs. Whitman became much attached to him. He was one day taken worse when at their house and never left it. They made him comfortable and attended to him as if he were a son or brother. He died very happy, bidding all good-by and thanking his friends for all their care of him. All gathered round the death-bed, and the scene was very impressive as he gave his last farewell to all around him.

NOTES

EDITOR'S NOTE: Catherine calls the illness "consumption" which is what today we would call tuberculosis. In the 19th century it was common to think that climate was a cause of many diseases. Now we know that tuberculosis is caused by a virus.

About this time the station had a visit from a band of Delaware Indians, under the leadership of

Tom Hill, who was very intelligent and could speak English as well as Cayuse. Dr. Whitman made a feast for them and invited the leading Cayuses and others. The indispensable item of an Indian feast was corn mush. A large kettle was suspended over a fire in the yard and the mush was made by putting in tallow and stirring in meal or flour. When cooked the kettle was taken indoors and placed on the floor. The doctor was master of ceremonies and the rest came in order of rank. The doctor and the chiefs dipped their spoons in the big kettle, but common people had dishes served and ate out of them. Some acted as waiters. They had tea, sweetened. We children were looking on, and it amused us to see what a quantity of sugar they used—all that the tea could hold. It was evening and the family occupied a bench on one side of the big room, which was crowded. It was well lighted with candles, and they ate in silence, except the sipping noise peculiar to Indians eating. Their performances at the trencher were so amusing to us that occasionally Mrs. Whitman had to send us outdoors to have our laugh out. When the feast was over the room was cleared and put in order for the speech. Tom Hill delivered an address that lasted two hours and was quite eloquent. We could understand the Cayuse talk, but the Indians did not know it. We were not allowed to learn it, and kept as much as possible away from the Indians, but constantly hearing the language spoken, we could not help but learn the meaning of it, though we could not speak it well. After the massacre they soon found out that we understood their talk. Mrs. Whitman always treated them politely and kindly, thanking them for every little favor they did her.

NOTES

EDITOR'S NOTE: Catherine Sager notes that Tom Hill was a Delaware Indian. Originally the Delaware (also known as "Lenape") lived in the mid-Atlantic region, but they were gradually forced westward as white settlement increased in the colonial era. However, the number of Delaware in Oregon Country was likely very small. Tom Hill and a few others came west as trappers, and also served as scouts on some of the first white expeditions in the west.

The next spring Mr. Rogers was away much of the time at the Spokane mission, conducted by Messrs. Walker and Eells. Dr. Whitman was absent at the saw mill or breaking up land for the Indians and plotting in their crops. Mrs. Whitman and the girls spent the time at home and found enough to employ them to prevent feeling lonesome. We studied botany with her and rambled over the country in search of flowers and plants.

A bad man was named Tam-a-has, meaning murderer, as he had once killed a man. One day the doctor was at work in his field when this man rode up and ordered him, peremptorily, to go and grind a grist for him. When the doctor objected to his talking and acting so, he said he could grind it for himself, and started for the mill. The doctor could walk across sooner and did so. Tam-a-has came at him there with a club, but saw an iron bar in his hand.

They had a serious time of it, both with words and blows, but the iron bar was a full match for the club, and Tam-a-has finally agreed to behave himself and have his grist ground. Exhausted in body and mind, the doctor came to the house and threw himself down, saying that if they would only say so he would gladly leave, for he was tired almost beyond endurance.

Tam-a-has (also Tamáhas or Tomakus)

It is hardly possible to conceive of a greater change than Dr. Whitman had worked in the life of the Cayuses. They now had growing fields, could have good homes, a mill to grind their meal, and they were taught things of the greatest use, yet some of them could not realize that he was unselfish in all this.

The following winter was very cold, the coldest ever known in the country and the Indians charged the whites with bringing the cold weather upon them. Old Jimmy, a Catholic Indian, claimed the power of working miracles, and said he brought the cold upon them to punish them for their unbelief and wickedness. They paid him liberally to bring about a change, and finally a thaw did come and he claimed all the merit of it.

The doctor made his fall visit to the valley, bringing back something for each one of us. He always remembered the children when he went to the valley, and brought us all some token of his love. He piloted the emigrants by a nearer and better route to The Dalles, and learned with apprehension that the last of the train were afflicted with measles and whooping cough. He knew they would spread through the native camps and feared the consequences. None of his own family had had the measles and but few of the others.

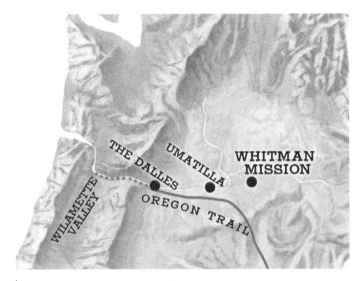

Map of places mentioned by Catherine Sager.

NOTES

EDITOR'S NOTE: The preceding map shows some of the places mentioned by Catherine Sager. What she calls "The Valley" was the Willamette Valley, where most Oregon-bound settlers were heading. There was a settlement there —supplied by ships—where the Whitmans might get certain supplies. The Dalles ("The" is part of the name) was the furthest west wagons could go at that time. At The Dalles, settlers would need to board rafts for the remainder of the trip to the Willamette Valley.

This fall brother John had his horse saddled to return to The Dalles to reside, but at Mr. Whitman's earnest request he consented to remain Had he gone there he might now be living! Laying aside his gun, he now devoted himself to his studies. He rose early, at 4 o'clock, and wrote, but I never knew what he wrote about, as the papers were all destroyed after the massacre.

The measles were among the natives, and in the doctor's absence Mrs. Whitman was their physician. All arrangements were made for the winter, teachers were employed, and all things were in order. The emigration had brought a Canadian half-breed named Jo Lewis, who was so disagreeable that they refused to let him travel farther in their company. Dr. Whitman reluctantly gave him some work. He tried to send him below with a company, but in a few days he was back again, so the doctor reluctantly engaged him for the winter. He was destitute of clothes and was supplied. We all disliked him, but he was well used and kindly treated. Yet this wretch laid the careful plans and told the terrible lies that led to the massacre, and took an active part in murder and robbery.

CHAPTER
TWO
WAIILATPU MASSACRE 1847

IN THE FALL OF 1847 THE EMIGRATION OVER the mountains brought the measles. It spread among the Indians, and owing to their manner of living it proved very fatal. It was customary for emigrant families who arrived late, to winter at the station, and some seven or eight families had put up there to spend the winter of 1847. Among the arrivals was a half-breed named Jo Lewis, who had joined the emigration at Fort Hall. Much against his will the doctor admitted this person into his family for the winter. We none of us liked him; he seemed surly and morose. There was also a Frenchman named Joseph Stanfield who had been in the doctor's employ since the year 1845. Up to the year 1847 the Protestant missions had been the only religious influence among the Indians. In the fall of this year the Catholic Church established missions among them, and the teachings of the two clashed. The Indian mind is so constructed that he cannot reconcile the different isms, consequently they became much worked up on the subject. Many long talks occurred between them and Dr. Whitman in reference to the two religious systems.

NOTES

EDITOR'S NOTE: It's important to put Catherine's statements in historical context. While her understanding of the "Indian Mind" seems strange—perhaps even racist —it was a common perception in that era. In truth, the Whitmans and the other missionaries in the region had a much more caring attitude toward native peoples than most other Euro-Americans. The Whitmans saw native people as children of God, and risked much to serve them. That said, the Whitmans assumed that the way to "help" the Cayuse was to make them more like Euro-Americans —a strategy that was doomed. In contrast to the Whitmans, the other nearby missionaries—the Spaldings —took greater effort to understand the native culture, beginning with the Nez Perce language.
They developed a written script for the Nez Perce tongue, and translated parts of the Bible into their native language. Many Nez Perce were baptized, and became Christians.

Owing to the sickness and these other causes, the natives began to show an insolent and hostile feeling. It was now late in the season and the weather was very inclement. Whitman's large family were all sick, and the disease was raging fearfully among the Indians, who were rapidly dying. I saw from five to six buried daily. The field was open for creating mischief, and the two Joes improved it. Jo Lewis was the chief agent; his cupidity had been awakened, and he and his associate expected to reap a large spoil. A few days previous to the massacre, Mr. Spaulding arrived at the station accompanied by his daughter, ten years old. She was the second child born of white parents west of the Rocky Mountains, Dr. Whitman's child being the first. She had lived her ten years of life among the natives, and spoke the language fluently.

Saturday, after his arrival, Mr. Spaulding accompanied Dr. Whitman to the Umatilla to visit the Indians there, and hold a meeting for worship with them upon the Sabbath. They rode nearly all night in a heavy rain. Dr. Whitman spent the next day visiting the sick, and returned to the lodge where Mr. Spaulding was staying, late in the afternoon, nearly worn out with fatigue. The condition of his family made it imperative that he should return home, so arrangements were made for Mr. Spaulding to remain a few days on the Umatilla to visit among and preach to the Indians.

As Dr. Whitman was mounting his horse to leave, Stickas, a friendly Christian Indian, who was the owner of the lodge, came out and told him that "Jo Lewis is making trouble: that he was telling his (Stickas) people that the doctor and Mr. Spaulding were poisoning the Indians so as to give their country to his own people." He said: "I do not believe him, but some do, and I fear they will do you harm; you had better go away for awhile until my people have better hearts."

Doctor Whitman arrived at home about 10 o'clock that night, having ridden twenty-five miles after sundown. He sent my two brothers, who were sitting up with the sick, to bed, saying that he would watch the remainder of the night. After they had retired he examined the patients one after the other. (I also was lying sick at the time.) Coming to Helen, he spoke and told his wife, who was lying on the bed, that Helen was dying. He sat and watched her for some time, when she rallied and seemed better. I had noticed that he seemed to be troubled when he first came home, but concluded that it was anxiety in reference to the sick children.

Taking a chair, he sat down by the stove and requested his wife to arise, as he wished to talk with her. She complied, and he related to her what Stickas had told him that day; also that he had learned that the Indians were holding councils every night. After conversing for some time his wife retired to another room, and the doctor kept his lonely watch. Observing that I was restless, he surmised that I had overheard the conversation. By kind and soothing words he allayed my fears and I went to sleep. I can see it all now and remember just how he looked.

The fatal 29th of November dawned a cold, foggy morning. It would seem as though the sun was afraid to look upon the bloody deed the day was to bring forth, and that nature was weeping over the wickedness of man. Father's (Dr. Whitman) brow was serene, with no trace of the storm that had raged in his breast during the night. He was somewhat more serious than usual. Most of the children were better, only three being dangerous; two of these afterwards died. We saw nothing of mother (Mrs. Whitman). One of the girls put some breakfast on a plate and carried it to her. She was sitting with her face buried in her handkerchief, sobbing bitterly. Taking the food, she motioned the child to leave. The food was there, untouched, next morning.

An Indian child had died during the night, and was to be brought to the station for burial. While awaiting the coming of the corpse, Dr. Whitman sat reading and conversing with his assistant, Mr. Rogers, upon the difficulties that seemed to surround him, the discontent of the Indians, the Catholics forcing themselves upon him, and the insinuations of Jo Lewis. He made plans for conciliating the natives and for improving their condition. He said that the Bishop was coming to see him in a few days and he thought that then he could get the

Indians to give him leave to go away in the spring, adding:

"If things do not clear up by that time I will move my family below."

Being informed of the arrival of the corpse, he arose, and after calling his wife and giving her directions in regard to the sick children, he wended his way to the graveyard.

A beef had to be killed for the use of the station, and my brother Francis, accompanied by Jo Stanfield, had gone early to the range and driven it in, and three or four men were dressing it near the grist mill, which was running, grinding grists for the Indians.

This artist's rendering shows the locations of the buildings at the mission. The Whitmans lived in the Mission House on the far right.

Upon the return from the funeral, the doctor remarked that none but the relatives were at the burying, although large numbers were assembled near by; but it might be owing to the beef being killed, as it was their custom to gather at such times. His wife requested him to go upstairs and see Miss Bewley, who was quite sick. He complied, returning shortly with a troubled look on his countenance. He crossed the room to a sash door that fronted the mill, and stood for some moments drumming upon the glass with his fingers. Turning around, he said:

"Poor Lorinda is in trouble and does not know the cause. I found her weeping, and she said there was a presentment of evil on her mind that she could not overcome. I will get her some medicine, and, wife, you take it up to her, and try and comfort her a little, for I have failed in the attempt."

As he said this he walked to the medicine case and was making a selection. His wife had gone to the pantry for milk for one of the children; the kitchen was full of Indians, and their boisterous manner alarmed her. She fled to the sitting room, bolting the door in the face of the savages who tried to pass in. She had not taken her hand from the lock when the Indians rapped and asked for the doctor. Just before the attack, Narcissa Whitman went into the kitchen.

There she was surprised to find a group of agitated Cayuse.

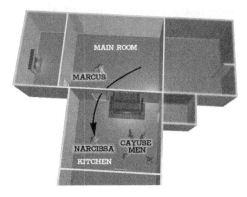

EDITOR'S NOTE: We can piece together this critical moment from a number of reports. Marcus Whitman sat down in the main room; Narcissa was bathing Catherine and her sister in the same room. Then Narcissa got up to get some milk from the pantry, which meant she had to pass through the kitchen. Surprised to see the Cayuse men in the kitchen, she quickly returned to the main room.

Dr. Whitman told his wife to bolt the door after him; she did so. Listening for a moment, she seemed to be reassured, crossed the room and took up the youngest child. She sat down with this child in her arms.

NOTES

EDITOR'S NOTE: After Narcissa left the kitchen and returned to the main room, Marcus went into the kitchen and told Narcissa to lock the door behind him. He know something was wrong.

Just then Mrs. Osborn came in from an adjoining room and sat down. This was the first time this lady had been out of her room for weeks, having been very ill. She had scarcely sat down when we were all startled by an explosion that seemed to shake the house. The two women sprang to their feet and stood with white faces and distended eyes. The children rushed out doors, some of them without clothes, as we were taking a bath. Placing the child on the bed, Mrs. Whitman called us back and started for the kitchen, but changing her mind, she fastened the door and told Mrs. Osborn to go to her room and lock the door, at the same time telling us to put on our clothes. All this happened much quicker than I can write it. Mrs. Whitman then began to walk the floor, wringing her hands, saying, "Oh, the Indians! the Indians! they have killed my husband, and I am a widow!" She repeated this many times. At this moment Mary Ann, who was in the kitchen, rushed around the house and came in at a door that was not locked.

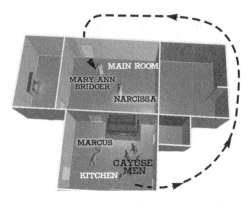

The path that Mary Ann Bridger takes to warn Narcissa.

Mary Ann's face was deathly white; we gathered around her and inquired if father was dead. She replied, "Yes."

NOTES

EDITOR'S NOTE: At this point Marcus Whitman was not actually dead, but he was mortally wounded.

Just then a man from the beef came in at the same door, with his arm broken. He said, "Mrs. Whitman, the Indians are killing us all." This roused her to action. The wounded man was lying upon the floor calling for water. She brought him a pitcherful from another room, locked all the doors, then unlocking that door, she went into the kitchen. As she did so several emigrant women with their small children rushed in.

EDITOR'S NOTE: There would be no fight when Narcissa re-entered the kitchen, because the Cayuse had run outside to continue the battle on the grounds.

Mrs. Whitman was trying to drag her husband in; one of the women went to her aid, and they brought him in. He was fatally wounded, but conscious. The blood was streaming from a gunshot wound in the throat. Kneeling over him she implored him to speak to her. To all her questions he whispered "yes" or "no," as the case might be. Mrs. Whitman would often step to the sash door and look out through the window to see what was going on out of doors, as the roar of guns showed us that the bloodthirsty fiends were not yet satisfied. At such times she would exclaim: "Oh, that Jo Lewis is doing it all!" Several times this wretch came to the door and tried to get into the room where we were. When Mrs. Whitman would ask, "What do you want, Jo?" he would run away. Looking out we saw Mr. Rogers running toward the house, hotly pursued by Indians. He sprang against the door, breaking out two panes of glass. Mrs. Whitman opened the door, and let him in, and closed it in the face of his pursuers, who, with a yell, turned to seek other victims. Mr. Rogers was shot through the wrist and tomahawked on the head; seeing the doctor lying upon the floor, he asked if he was dead, to which the doctor replied, "No."

The school teacher, hearing the report of the guns in the kitchen, ran down to see what had happened; finding the door fastened, he stood for a moment, when Mrs. Whitman saw him and motioned for him to go back. He did so, and had reached the stairs leading to the schoolroom, when he was seized by a savage who had a large butcher knife. Mr. Sanders struggled and was about to get away when another burly savage came to the aid of the first. Standing by Mrs. Whitman's side, I watched the horrid strife until, sickened, I turned away. Just then a bullet came through the window, piercing Mrs. Whitman's shoulder. Clasping her hands to the wound, she shrieked with pain, and then fell to the floor. I ran to her and tried to raise her up. She said, "Child, you cannot help me, save yourself." We all crowded around her and began to weep. She commenced praying for us, "Lord, save these little ones." She repeated this over many times. She also prayed for her parents, saying: "This will kill my poor mother."

The women now began to go upstairs, and Mr. Rogers pushed us to the stairway. I was filled with agony at the idea of leaving the sick children and refused to go. Mr. Rogers was too excited to speak, so taking up one of the children, he handed her to me, and motioned for me to take her up. I passed her to some one else, turned and took another, and then the third and ran up myself.

N O T E S

> EDITOR'S NOTE: The upstairs room was directly above the main room in the house.

Mr. Rogers then helped mother to her feet, and brought her upstairs and laid her on the bed. He then knelt in prayer, and while thus engaged, the crashing of doors informed us that the work of death was accomplished out of doors, and our time had come. The wounded man, whose name was Kimball, said that if we had a gun to hold over the banisters it might keep them away. There happened to be an old broken gun in the room, and this was placed over the railing. By this time they were smashing the door leading to the stairway. Having accomplished this they retired. All was quiet for awhile, then we heard footsteps in the room below, and a voice at the bottom of the stairway called Mr. Rogers. It was an Indian, who represented that he had just come; he would save them if they would come down. After a good deal of parleying he came up. I told mother that I had seen him killing the teacher, but she thought I was mistaken. He said that they were going to burn the house, and that we must leave it. I wrapped my little sister up and handed her to him with the request that he would carry her. He said that they would take Mrs. Whitman away and then come back for us. Then all left save the children and Mr. Kimball. When they reached the room below mother was laid upon a settee and carried out into the yard by Mr. Rogers and Jo Lewis. Having reached the yard, Jo dropped his end of the settee, and a volley of bullets laid Mr. Rogers, mother and brother Francis, bleeding and dying, on the ground. While the Indians were holding a council to decide how to get Mrs. W. and Mr. Rogers into their hands, Jo Lewis had been sent to the schoolroom to get the school children. They had hid in the attic, but were ferreted out and brought to the kitchen, where they were placed in a row to be shot. But the chief relented, and said they should not be hurt; but my brother Francis was killed soon after. My oldest brother was shot at the same time the doctor was.

N O T E S

EDITOR'S NOTE: Historians believe that 72 people were at the mission on the day of the killings (Nov. 29, 1847). Fourteen were killed, including both Marcus and Narcissa Whitman. About 50 women and children were taken hostage, and ransomed about 2 weeks later.

Night had now come, and the chief made a speech in favor of sparing the women and children, which was done, and they all became prisoners. Ten ghastly, bleeding corpses lay in and around the house. Mr. Osborn's family had secreted themselves under the floor, and escaped during the night, and after great hardships reached Fort Walla Walla. One other man escaped to this fort, but was never heard of again. Another fled to Mr. Spaulding's station; Mr. Kimball was killed the next day; Mr. Spaulding remained at Umatilla until Wednesday, and was within a few miles of the doctor's station when he learned the dreadful news. He fled, and after great suffering, reached his station, which had been saved by the presence of mind and shrewdness of his wife. Mr. Canfield was wounded, but concealing himself until night, he fled to Mr. Spaulding's station.

The manner of the attack on Dr. Whitman I learned afterward from the Indians. Upon entering the kitchen, he took his usual seat upon a settee which was between the wall and the cook stove; an Indian began to talk to him in reference to a patient the doctor was attending. While thus engaged an Indian struck him from behind on the head with a tomahawk; at the same moment two guns were discharged, one at the doctor, and the other at brother John, who was engaged in winding twine for the purpose of making brooms. The men at the beef were set upon; Mr. Kimball had his arm broken by a bullet, and fled to the doctor's house. Mr. Hoffman fought bravely with an axe; he split the foot of the savage who first struck the doctor, but was overpowered. Mr. Canfield was shot, the bullet entering his side, but he made his escape. The miller fell at his post. Mr. Hall was laying the upper floor in a building; leaping to the ground, he wrested a gun from an Indian, and fled to the fort. He was never seen or heard of afterwards, and it is surmised that he was murdered there. The tailor was sitting upon his table sewing, an Indian stepped in, shot him with a pistol, and then went out; he died at midnight after great suffering. Night came and put an end to the carnival of blood.

The November moon looked down, bright and cold, upon the scene, nor heeded the groans of the dying who gave forth their plaints to the chill night air. Mr. Osborn's family were concealed where they could hear Mr. Rogers's words as he prayed to that Saviour whom he had loved and served for many years. His last words were: "Come, Lord Jesus, come quickly!" The clock tolled the midnight hour ere death came to the relief of these victims of savage brutality. The dead bodies lay where they fell from Monday night until Wednesday, when the Christian Indians, among whom the doctor and his wife had labored for eleven years, and from whom the natives had received nothing but kindness, gave consent to have them buried, but not one of them would help in the task. Jo Stanfield was set at the work. A grave three feet deep and wide enough to receive the eleven victims was dug, and the bodies placed in it. Wolves excavated the grave and devoured the remains. The volunteers who went up to fight the Indians gathered up the bones, placed them in a wagon box, and again buried them, and this is all the burial these martyrs of Americanism in Oregon have ever received.

CHAPTER
THREE
IN CAPTIVITY

NOTES

EDITOR'S NOTE: After the initial attack, many of the children and the wounded adults escaped to an upstairs room. Without any working weapons, they were eventually persuaded by the Cayuse to assemble downstairs—with a promise they would not be harmed. However, 10-year-old Eliza Spalding, who was fluent in the Cayuse language, understood that tribal leaders were debating whether to kill all the survivors. The decision was made to spare the children, but Narcissa was taken outside and killed. The others scurried upstairs. This is where Catherine picks up the story.

THE NIGHT OF NOVEMBER 29, 1847, FOUND me, a girl of thirteen years sitting in company with two sisters and two half-breed girls upon a bed in the chamber of a large adobe house. On the floor lay a white man with his arm broken. A fearful scene had been enacted during the day; savage fury had swept over Whitman's station, and we thought that we only of all who awoke to busy life in the morning remained alive. When the woman who had supplied the place of mother to us for several years had been induced, by what proved to be false promises, to leave for a place of safety, we expected soon to join her and accompany her to the fort, but the roar of musketry that soon shook the house left us in utter despair. We were convinced of the treachery of the savages, and hope, which a moment before had lifted our hearts to almost buoyancy, now fled entirely. The wounded man exclaimed, "Treachery! Treachery! Children, prepare for the worst."

With hearts filled with fright, we awaited the coming of the murderers, and cold chills seized me as I thought of the dreadful knives I had seen them using upon their victims. During the day we were too much palsied with terror to even cry, but stood listening with pale cheeks and distended eyes to every move below. Soon we heard the savages split- ting kindling; then one called for fire We now thought our doom was to die by fire and that our home would be our funeral pile; but, strange to say, I experienced a feeling of relief at the thought— anything rather than meet again those fierce savages with their knives.

We listened in vain for the roar of the flames; we heard instead some one addressing the Indians. The speech continued for some time, and then all was still. They had evidently left the premises. Three of the children were very sick; their clothing was wet with blood from lying on the bed with Mrs. Whitman after she was wounded. We had no fire or light, and we did not even think to get warmth by wrapping bedding around us. I tried to soothe the children to sleep, reasoning to myself that if we could lose consciousness in slumber that the roof of the burning house would fall upon us and we would not know it. We still thought that they would fire the building. The sick children were suffering for water, and begged for it continually. I remembered taking up a cupful the day previous for a young lady who was lying ill. I directed my sister where to find it, but in searching for it in the dark she knocked it down and spilt it. The disappointment seemed to add to their thirst, and their pleadings for a drink were heartrending. I begged of the wounded man to let them have some from a pitcher he had brought up with him, but he said it was bloody and not fit to drink. The hours dragged slowly along, and from exhaustion the children fell asleep one after the other, until the man and I were the only ones awake. I sat upon the side of the bed, watching hour after hour, while the horrors of the day passed and repassed before my mind. I had always been very much afraid of the dark, but now I felt that the darkness was a protection to us and I prayed that it might always remain so. I dreaded the coming of the daylight; again I would think, with a shudder, of the dead lying in the room below. I heard the cats racing about and squalling, with a feeling that seemed to freeze the blood in my veins. I remember yet how terrible the striking of the clock sounded. Occasionally Mr. Kimball would ask if I were asleep.

Hours were passed in this manner, when sleep came and locked my senses in its friendly embrace. About 3 o'clock I awoke with a start. As I moved my hand I felt a shaggy head and shrieked with alarm. Kimball spoke and told me not to be alarmed, that it was he. He had become cold and tired lying on the floor, and was sitting up to rest, but had to lean against the bed because he was so faint. We conversed for some time, our voices awakening the children, who renewed their calls for water. Day began to break, and Mr. K. told me to take a sheet off the bed and bind up his arm, and he would try and get them some. I arose, stiff with cold, and with a dazed, uncertain feeling. He repeated his request. I said, "Mother would not like to have the sheets torn up." Looking at me, he said: "Child, don't you know your mother is dead, and will never have any use for the sheets?" I seemed to be dreaming, and he had to urge me to comply with his request. I took a sheet from the bed and tore off some strips, which, by his directions, I wound around his arm. He then told me to put a blanket around him, as he might faint on the way and not be able to get up, and would suffer with the cold. Taking a pair of blankets from the bed, I put them around him, tying them around the waist with a strip off the sheets. I then placed his hat on his head and he went downstairs. We waited long for him, but he came not, and we never saw him again alive.

NOTES

EDITOR'S NOTE: The reason Kimball wrapped himself in blankets was to camouflage himself as an Indian. His goal was to go down to the river for water and bring it back to the children. He made it to the river safely, but when he returned with the water, he was noticed by the Cayuse and killed.

It was now fully light, and we heard the Indians arriving. They were calling Mr. Osborn, and we heard utensils jingling, and concluded that Mr. Osborn's family had been spared and were getting breakfast. Soon we heard approaching footsteps and some one ascending the stairs. We huddled together and almost held our breath, not knowing what would happen to us. It was Jo Lewis and several Indians. He told us that we would not be hurt; that he was going to take us to the fort as soon as he could get up a team. Saying this he left. The Indians remained; they were mostly young men; they asked me what made the children cry. I replied, They are hungry, and want water. One of them went for water and one for food. They soon returned, one bearing a bowl of water and the other a plate of cold victuals. They directed me to gather up our clothes in readiness to go to the fort. Bringing a large basket for me to put them in, they also brought a loaf of bread for me to put in, saying we would get hungry. We had none of us yet ventured downstairs. The water was consumed and the children were begging for more. I tried to get some of the natives to go for more, but they seemed to think they had done enough and refused. I could not bear to hear the piteous calls for water, so taking the bowl I went down. I found my shoes where I had left them the day before; putting them on I went to the river after water. Having obtained it I was returning. Some Indians were sitting upon the fence; one of them pointed his gun at me. I was terribly frightened, but walked on. One sitting near him knocked the gun up and it went off in the air. I went to the children with the water. There were no Indians in the house, and we ventured down to take a look at things. The Indians had spread quilts over the corpses. Mary Ann, my sister, lifted the quilt from Dr. Whitman's face, and said: "Oh, girls, come and see father." We did so, and saw a sight we will never forget. Passing into the kitchen we found the mangled body of brother John. We were crying bitterly when Joe Stanfield stepped out of the pantry and ordered us to hush; that "the Indians would be mad and kill us if they saw us taking on so." The savages were now crowding in, and we again retreated upstairs. Jo Stanfield had told us to go over to the other house, as the other women and children were there, but we were afraid to leave our own retreat. As we passed through the sitting-room many native women were in it; they wept over us, and loaded us down with clothing which they were collecting. The Indians came up and urged us to leave, so mustering courage I took one child and my sister one. As Mary Ann was not strong enough to carry the other one, and would not stay with her, we were under the necessity of leaving her, promising to return as soon as we could. Upon reaching the room below we found the kitchen to be full of savages, and were afraid to pass through, so we went out through the Indian room. At the outer door we passed the corpse of Francis. We were met about half way by the girls; for several moments we all wept, and then some of them relieved us of our loads. On reaching the house I fainted. As soon as consciousness returned I informed them that Helen was still at the house, and I would have to return for her. Several volunteered to go with me. We found her screaming with fright and calling for me.

We were now captives of a horde of savages. The house we were held captive in was a large, square adobe building, containing five rooms, one being a bedroom and the others large living rooms. Each of these rooms had two families living in it. The Indians supplied us with plenty of food. Every morning early they would come from their village, a mile or two away, and stay until late at night. We had to prepare food for them, of which they would make us eat first, for fear that we had put poison in it. The women seldom came around. When night came and the beds were made down, the Indians would take possession of them, and we would frequently have to sit up until midnight before they would leave the house.

NOTES

EDITOR'S NOTE: At this point, Catherine and about 50 others were hostages. There was still talk among the Cayuse about killing them, but chief Tiloukaikt was a voice of moderation.

On the 5th of December my little sister, six years old, died; three days afterwards Helen died. There were two young men at the station who were sick with a fever at the time of the massacre. These men were not killed at that time. One of them spent the night of the 29th of November alone in his room, not knowing that any one else was alive aside from himself. They had both been removed to the house where we were staying. One evening we were startled by the savages attacking these men as they lay in their bed. We all rushed outside, supposing that we were all to be killed. An Indian told us to come back, that only the two were to be killed. Late that evening there was a knock at the door, and a voice in English called the name of one of the young women named Mary Smith. It proved to be her father, who with his family and another family had arrived from the saw mill, where they were employed. They had been brought down to be murdered, but word had come from the fort that no more Americans were to be slaughtered. It came too late to save the two young men, who had been dead several hours. These men were set at running the grist mill.

One evening an Indian came to the house and seemed to be looking for some one. We learned that it was Miss Bewley. She was sick with the ague, and was lying in bed.

He went to the bed and began to fondle over her. She sprang up and sat down behind the stove. He sat down by her and tried to prevail upon her to be his wife. She told him that he had a wife, and that she

NOTES

"The ague" is a term for a feverish disease. It eventually became a term for a particular type of feverish disease— malaria. But it is doubtful Miss Bewley had malaria.

would not have him. Finding that persuasion nor threats availed, he seized her and dragged her out of the house, and tried to place her upon his horse; he failed in this also. She told him that she would tell the chief of his conduct the next day. He said he would not let her do so. She replied that she would call loud enough for him to hear her and come to see what was the matter. He tried to stop her screams by placing his hand over her mouth. The contest lasted for some time, when, becoming enraged, he threw her with violence upon the ground. After perpetrating his hellish designs upon her, he ordered her to go to the house. The poor, heartbroken girl came in, shaking with agitation. One of the women sent Eliza and I to get some medicine for her. It was in another room; the fiend was in there, and wanted to know what we wanted of the medicine. We told him it was for a sick child. We carried it in, well pleased with our ruse. A few days after this a chief of the Umatillas sent for and carried Miss B. there and held her as his wife. The evening after she left the other came with a wagon and a team. He had ropes and men to assist him to carry her to his lodge.

N O T E S

EDITOR'S NOTE: After these events, Lorinda Bewley was taken 25 miles to the lodge of a chief named Five Crows where he forced her to be his "wife." Eventually she was ransomed and lived until 1899.

Previous to this the Indians had held a council to

decide what to do with their prisoners. Many speeches were made; the savage mentioned above said he could see no use in bothering with them; the easiest and quickest way to get rid of them was to kill them. He sat down, and a Nez Perce arose and gave him such a scathing rebuke that he cowed down and had no more to say. They decided to keep us during the winter, and then send us below in the spring. We were informed of this, with the assurance that we would all be killed if our countrymen attempted our rescue. A few evenings after this another council was held, at which we were required to be present. This council was for the purpose of setting before the young women the policy of taking chiefs for their husbands to protect them from violence. The poor girls had to submit to the decrees of their captors. The remembrance of these things takes all admiration for the noble red man from those who had the experience. Our captors kept us busy making them shirts out of the goods taken at the station—we knew that the Indians were planning an expedition to The Dalles. It was no unusual thing for one to come and demand a shirt made against a set time, as he was going to The Dalles. We would make the shirt, he would come and get it, bid us good-bye, and leave, but in a day or so be back with another shirt to make. We learned that this was a ruse adopted to have their sewing done first. Sometimes it was done to see if we would sew upon the Sabbath. One Sabbath evening a fellow came and wanted us to make him a shirt that evening. We refused, telling him it was the Sabbath. He became very abusive, so we commenced the shirt, and seeing this he left. We then laid it aside, and next day complained to the chief, and he forbid them bringing us work to do upon the Sabbath.

The Indians generally stayed around until near midnight. After they would leave some of the vagabonds would come in and harass us and manage to frighten us thoroughly for their own amusement. To prevent this we adopted the plan of hiring some of the influential men to stay with us until l or 2 o'clock. The one who oftenest performed this service was Beardy. He had remained in the lodge upon the day of the massacre till late in the day, when he came upon the scene and made a touching appeal for the lives of the women and children. He was a professor of religion and was regarded as a good Indian. The ladies were in the habit of setting him a lunch before he left. One of them had baked some pies made of dried peaches, and which were kept hid from the other natives. These particularly suited old Beardy's taste, and notwithstanding he had eaten several hearty meals during the day, he partook freely of them. After reaching home his stomach rebelled and rejected the load. Seeing the fruit thrown from his stomach, he mistook it for blood and concluded that we had poisoned him, and vowed that our lives should pay the forfeit. He was sick three days; on the fourth he came armed with a band of savages to wreak vengeance upon our defenseless heads. During the night an Indian woman had arrived from Fort Hall. Her husband was a white man, and she spoke the English language well. As soon as she heard of the massacre she started for the station, and her arrival was very opportune. She pleaded our cause with Beardy and convinced him that he alone was to blame —that he had only overeaten himself. He was very much ashamed of the affair, and used to laugh over it. It came near being a serious joke to us.

NOTES

The pie incident shows just how quickly a small misunderstanding could escalate. Unfortunately, this pattern was all too common in interactions between native and white peoples.

It was our custom to gather in some one of the rooms to spend the evenings; we felt better when thus together. One evening I was sitting by the fire in a room some distance from the one I occupied, when a stalwart savage came in, seized me by the arm and dragged me shrieking through the house to our room, which was empty at the time, excepting the sleeping children. Placing a chair, he told me to sit down; he then began to court me for his friend. The friend soon came in and I was compelled to listen to their love speeches. A half-breed present came in and told them not to try to carry me away. They said they did not intend to; they only wanted to amuse themselves. I could not see the fun, but sat shivering with fright and cold. I begged them to let me go to the fire; they refused and wrapped a blanket around me. They made my life a torment to me, and so afraid was I of being carried off by them that I was tempted to end my troubles by jumping into the mill pond. My fellow-prisoners sympathized with me, and laid many plans for eluding them. Jo Stanfield proposed that I should go to the straw stack and sleep, but this the women would not allow, as they were suspicious of him. Some proposed that I go to Jo Finlay's lodge in company with one of Mr. Young's sons. This was also abandoned. Mr. Young and his wife then laid a plan by which they thought I could elude them. During the day their extra beds were thrown upon the bedstead. In the evening the old gentleman was in the habit of lying on the front of the bedstead. The girls were to watch their chance, when the Indians would be out of the room, and take me in. I was then to get over behind the pile of bedding and lie down. A few evenings afterwards they came and the plan was carried out with complete success. I lay quiet, and although they searched the house, they failed to find me, and left, giving vent to their chagrin in loud whoops. Soon after one of them came again. I went to bed and was asleep, as was every one else. I felt some one pulling me by the arm; starting up, I confronted my enemy; he wanted me to sit by the fire with him; I refused. He tried coaxing and threats, but in my desperation I lost all fear of him, and fought with teeth and nails. He said if I would sit and talk with him he would go away, but I would not. The contest lasted for some time, then he raised his whip and said he would whip me, but I cared not, and still fought him, calling upon other Indians who were sleeping near to help me. They paid no heed, but the white men, getting tired of the row, jumped up, when he left and never came back. The Indians called me a brave girl, that would thus fight a man.

Knowing how treacherous the nature of the savages was, we lived in constant fear of their murdering us. We watched for their coming in the morning and only felt safe when they departed at night. It was my custom to take my sister, who was three years old and was prostrated by a long and severe illness, in my arms and sit down behind the stove every morning and thus await their coming, resolved to die with her in my arms should they murder us. Occasionally I would go over to my desolated home. What a scene was presented there!

Mutilated furniture, feathers, ashes, straw and blood, all commingled in one indiscriminate mass; desolation reigned where once had been peace and harmony. Amid all the anguish and turmoil of those dark days there would sometimes things occur that were ludicrous enough to make us for a moment forget sorrow and indulge in a hearty laugh. One day an Indian brave came riding to the house with a large map of the world thrown over his horse for a blanket. At another time the voices of the children would be heard singing hymns, accompanied by the natives. Oh, blessed childhood, that can thus throw off sorrow and gloom!

On the 26th of December word came that three boats had arrived at the fort. This news caused great excitement, both to captors and captives, and a messenger was dispatched to learn the particulars. In a few hours he returned with the information that the great chief of the Hudson's Bay Company had come and wanted the Indians to meet him in council next day. The greatest excitement prevailed among the captors and their captives. While the hope of rescue was feebly entertained, it was overshadowed by the thought of another terrible massacre, in which we would be the victims. Our captors left for their village, but in the course of a few hours returned in their hideous war paint and armed to the teeth. They remained a short time to finish their preparations, and then departed for the fort. It was just nightfall when they left.

The fort Catherine refers to is nearby Ft. Walla Walla, which itself did not have the resources to solve the hostage situation. So word was sent to the much larger outpost, Ft. Vancouver (pictured above), which was 250 miles east of the Whitman Mission. Word reached Ft. Vancouver on Dec. 6, about a week after the events. The next day, a rescue party departed, intending to negotiate the release of the hostages.

Oh, what anxious days those were; how slowly the hours seemed to drag along! On the evening of the second day we were overjoyed at receiving Miss Bewley again. She gave us a graphic account of her life during her absence. We slept but little that night, and as soon as daylight appeared we started for the fort. All of us wept as we drove away from that scene of suffering; wept for joy at our escape and for sorrow for those who had been slain and could not go with us. As we left an Indian woman came from a lodge near by and told us to hasten for our lives, that her people had repented and were coming to kill us. We made all speed we could, and as darkness came on the welcome walls of the fort loomed dimly before us and we were soon inside, but did not feel safe until a week afterwards, we reached the settlements. Thus ended our captivity among the Indians.

NOTES

Catherine skips a lot of details here, because she likely did not know how her release was secured. Peter Skene Ogden arrived from Fort Vancouver with 16 men—and a plan to rescue the hostages. Ogden was highly respected among the native peoples. He offered blankets, tobacco and guns in exchange for the hostages. It's important to note that the native leaders did not approve of the killings, and wanted peace with the whites, especially Ogden. They agreed to the exchange.

FIRST PIONEER GIRL IN THE WEST

ELIZA SPALDING

INTRODUCTION

Eliza Spalding was a friend of Catherine Sager's. They both went to school at the Whitman Mission, and both were present for the tragedy at Waiilatpu.

Unlike Catherine Sager —who went west at age 9— Eliza Spalding was born in Oregon Country. Her birth in 1837 made Eliza the very first pioneer girl to be born and grow up in the mountain west.

Based on an existing photo, this is an artist's rendering of what Eliza looked like at about 8-years-old.

Her story is unparalleled—and offers fascinating insights into the earliest days of the emigrants. Eliza's parents launched the Oregon Trail era with the original covered wagon trek in 1836. Settling in the region that is now the junction of Oregon, Washington, and Idaho, Eliza grew up among native peoples. She learned their language and understood their culture better than any pioneer girl of the era.

Eliza was at the Whitman Mission on the day of the fateful attacks that so profoundly changed the course of western history. Her telling of that story is uniquely valuable—even though she was just 10 years old—because she was the only survivor who spoke the language of the attackers. This first-person account is an eye-opening look at life in the early West.

Eliza's story is as fresh and readable today as the day it was written—a rare example of a historic document that can still engage modern readers, even children. This enhanced edition adds dozens of photos, maps, graphics, and notes to the original manuscript. The bonus material provides a layer of context that gives readers deeper insight into her compelling story.

One note to keep in mind: Eliza's mother was also named Eliza, which can be confusing when researching these two women. For that reason, they are sometimes referred to as Eliza Spalding Warren (daughter) and Eliza Hart Spalding (mother).

Michael Trinklein, editor

CHAPTER
ONE

I WAS BORN AT LAPWAI ON THE CLEARWATER River, near the present town of Lewiston, Idaho, November 15, 1837. My father, Henry Harmon Spalding, was born at Bath, New York, and my mother, Eliza Hart, was a native of Hartford, Connecticut.

After my father and mother were married they decided to give their lives to the cause of missions, and they chose the Osage Indians as their charges. This was before their meeting with Dr. Marcus Whitman. He was looking for somebody to accompany

NOTES

EDITOR'S NOTE: The United States was barely 50 years old at this time. There were no railroads in the mountain west; no farms; no white settlers. Millions of native people lived in the west, and most people assumed this would remain their land.

him on the long journey across the continent, and he finally persuaded my parents to give up the Osages and go to the Oregon territory.

They established their station at Lapwai. Their Indians, the Nez Perces, received them kindly, and from the very beginning showed a desire to learn the things that the white people had traveled so far to teach them. Doctor Whitman and his wife began their mission among the Cayuse Indians, about thirty miles from Fort Walla Walla in Washington; they were nearly one hundred and twenty miles from our home.

Lapwai (upper left) was a tiny outpost far from what was then the United States.

My memory of girlhood days extends back to the time I was five years old. I can see the little log house on the bank of the Clearwater, the hills that loom up on each side of the stream, the garden where we raised an abundance of things to eat, and the orchard that was just beginning to bear fruit when I reached that period in life to which memory now goes back.

The simple cabin the Spalding family lived in during their early years at Lapwai.

We were always among the Indians, as no day passed that several did not come to consult Father regarding the many things he was trying to teach them.

On the Sabbath the gatherings were of great interest to me. Father would preach to the tribe, and one of the natives would interpret all that he said. It was a strange audience. The Indians sat flat on the floor and listened patiently, and took the most serious sort of interest in Father's sermons. Their behavior through the devotional exercises was always splendid, and they never attempted to annoy the white man who had come among them. I can see them in the schoolroom, where Father and Mother were busy during several hours of the day. At times there would be as many as two hundred Indians to be instructed. They were in earnest about it too. Six or seven of them would often come to our cabin in the evening to get additional help with their lessons.

This photo of the area is from about 50 years after Eliza's childhood, but it gives you a sense of the landscape where she grew up.

Mother taught the girls carding, spinning and weaving, and general housework. As the Indian women are naturally adept at weaving they were delighted with the things she showed them, especially the bright colors of cloth she gave them to work with.

Father taught the men to cultivate and raise crops in the fields and gardens. Under his care they planted each year a large quantity of wheat. During harvest it was cut with hand sickles and bound into small bundles. The method of threshing was, of course, quite crude. The Indians brought the wheat to a big corral and spread it thickly over the ground. A bunch of wild horses were then turned into the enclosure and driven around until the grain was trampled from the wheat heads. When the wind was blowing, the trampled grain was tossed in the air, and in this primitive manner the wheat was winnowed and cleaned.

NOTES

EDITOR'S NOTE: It's not easy to get the edible part of the wheat—called the "kernel"—separated from the inedible part which is called the "chaff." So horses were used to stomp on the wheat to essentially rub off the outer parts, exposing the kernel. Then the mix would be tossed in the air. The lighter chaff would blow away, leaving a pile of kernels. The process Eliza describes is exactly how it had been done for thousands of years.

Eliza's father Henry Spalding (shown here later in life) believed native people needed to adopt the ways of European-Americans like himself. Henry had difficulty learning the Nez Perce language, and often lashed out in anger. This led to conflicts with the Nez Perce people, some of whom resented Spalding's attempts to change their culture. This was in stark contrast to his wife Eliza (who had the same name as her daughter who authored this book) who learned the native tongue and was respectful of Nez Perce culture.

CHAPTER
TWO

FATHER TOOK CONSIDERABLE PAINS TO erect the first gristmill of the country, and then taught the Indians how to use it, helping them as they brought the grain to be ground into flour. During the milling season the Indians poured in from their camps with their little cayuse ponies loaded to the very tails with sacks of grain. That always furnished an amusing sight for me.

One day as the Indians were bringing wheat to the mill a group of younger Indians took a notion that they could run things better than the old man in charge. So they knocked him down and pulled him out of the way, taking control of the mill. Father soon appeared on the scene, seized the leader and forced him from the building. This made the Indian angry, and he knocked Father down and began choking him. Mother ran screaming for help. The older Indians came up and stopped the trouble at once. The Indian who caused the excitement was sternly rebuked by his elders. One of the men said to Mother: "Do you not know that we will never let any one hurt Father Spalding? "

Nez Perce mother and child. As with any cultural group, there were differences of opinion about many matters, including whether the Spaldings were a benefit or a threat.

The thought has often occurred to me of how absolutely at the mercy of the Indians we were, and yet I never saw my parents show any signs of uneasiness. Father used to go away and leave Mother alone with the Indians for days. They seemed to be pleased with the confidence he had in them, and they took the greatest pains to see that Mother's every need was satisfied. Once, when she had been sick for a long time and we all feared that she would never recover, the Indians were most solicitous, and never a day passed that they did not ask about her condition. One of the old chiefs used to sit by her bedside and watch her quietly. He broke his stolid reserve at one time, and in his broken Indian manner said to her: "Oh, that I might be taken in your place and you could be spared to teach my people!"

EDITOR'S NOTE: Eliza's mother (also named Eliza) was one of the more extraordinary women in U.S. history. She and Narcissa Whitman were the first white women to cross the Rockies. Unlike many of the other early settlers, Eliza learned the language of the native people and didn't try to force the Nez Perce to conform to white ways of living. She singlehandedly developed a written language for the tribe and taught many to read and write. Tribal members loved her, and would protect and defend her whenever necessary. (While no images exist of Eliza's mother when she was young, this artists's rendering is based on images taken from later years and "de-aged" to show what she looked like during the 1830s)

CHAPTER
THREE

OFTEN DURING MY GIRLHOOD I WENT ON long horseback trips with Father. I was just seven years old when he took me with him to the Camas Prairie, about two days' ride from our home, at the base of the Blue Mountains near the present town of Grangeville. The Indian women were digging camas and "cowse" roots to be used during the winter for food. They used to make an expedition every autumn and collect large stores of the roots.

But the longest trip Father and I made was in 1845, when we rode horseback for more than five hundred miles into the Willamette Valley and on to the Pacific Coast. I was only eight years old. Father had some business to attend to and decided that I should go along for company.

Camas is a beautiful blue flower that grows in many valleys in the region. The root was an important food source for the New Perce people. Women would dig up the roots each year and store them for use through the winter (see above). Lewis and Clark had written about the roots—which gave the explorers indigestion because of the high fiber content.

We took plenty of time and enjoyed it all. At night we would camp near a clump of bushes and cook our meals over an open fire. We could make fifty miles a day and not be very tired. Of course we were thoroughly accustomed to long riding or I could not have endured it. We stopped at The Dalles for a few days to rest, and visited two missionary families there; I remember that I was very glad to talk with white friends once more. The trip over the Cascade Mountains was wonderful. I was delighted when we reached the large forest. It was the first big timber I had ever seen, and I marveled at the monstrous trees; they were so thick and the branches so dense that it seemed as dark as night while we were traveling through them. Some of our horses were stripped of their packs as they struggled through the matted undergrowth.

But crossing the mountain streams was the hardest work. Sometimes I thought the horses simply could not make it across the rushing torrents; they floundered over hidden rocks and boulders, and, after much perilous slipping, finally made all the dangerous fords without much damage. It was exciting sport, rather strenuous for a little girl of eight years.

Some of the places Eliza visited on her journey.

At last we came to Oregon City and stopped for a short rest. I don't remember the exact number of houses; perhaps there were twelve. But I know they

seemed mighty large and fine to me; they were the
first I had ever seen with paint on them. They
seemed almost like palaces to my girlish imagina-
tion; my home was nothing but a log cabin without a
sign of paint.

Oregon City at about the time Eliza would have visited with
her father. This was before large number of pioneers were
traveling west on the Oregon Trail, so the city was still very
small.

From Oregon City we took rowboats on the
Willamette River and went as far as Portland. There
was one log house where the big coast city is today!
Farther on we stopped at Fort Vancouver and then at
Astoria, with one little shack on the side of the hill.
A warship was anchored near there and we went on
board. That was my first view of the great Pacific.

On the whole it was a most wonderful trip, as I

saw for the first time all sorts of entrancing sights. On the way back I was taken ill and Father had to carry me for a long distance on the saddle in front of him.

As a girl I was not allowed to make constant companions of the Indian children. Mother was determined that I should not grow up a savage, even if we did live in a wild and savage place. I had little household duties to perform, and I was always impressed with one's responsibility in life. The older Indians were quite proud of the first white baby that was born among them and they did everything they could think of to make me a true child of the West. 1 was a great pet with them. They taught me to swim and ride horseback, and gave me careful instruction in the many secrets of Nature that an Indian understands thoroughly to the white man's mystification. I learned the Nez Perce language, and later acted frequently as interpreter.

NOTES

EDITOR'S NOTE: Please excuse Eliza's use of words like "savage." At the time, white people knew almost nothing of native culture and often used unfortunate language. However, note that Eliza's actions reflected a deep caring for the Nez Perce people. In the 1840s, she understood the Northwest tribes better than any pioneer girl in America—thanks to her unique firsthand experience.

When I was nine years old I was sent to Doctor

Whitman's station to attend the school that had been started there. Emigrant families on the way to the Willamette country formed a habit of stopping at the Whitman mission during the winter.

Of course there were a number of children along, and it was deemed advisable to organize a school for their benefit. As there were not enough children in any other part of the country that was the only school near us. It was one hundred and twenty miles from our home. On the first trip Father was too busy to take me, and he entrusted me to

Dr. Marcus Whitman, who—with his wife Narcissa—operated the Whitman Mission.

the care of Matilda, a faithful Indian woman who had helped Mother with her work at home. That trip certainly shows that my parents placed implicit confidence in the tribe. We traveled on horseback and took a pack-horse to carry provisions. We were three nights on the way, and we camped wherever darkness overtook us. I shall never forget the tender care of that dear old Matilda. Each evening she unsaddled the horses and hobbled them to prevent their straying off; then she built the fire and cooked the supper. Every night I lay awake and listened to the howling of the coyotes and the big gray wolves. I wasn't afraid of the coyotes, but the wolves were always a cause for worry. They did more than howl, and we were never sure that our horses would be alive when we awoke the next morning. I remember how faithfully Matilda followed our family custom of evening prayers; I don't believe she would have slept all night had she gone to bed without the usual worship. That has always seemed to me a great tribute to the work of Father and Mother.

NOTES

EDITOR'S NOTE: This remarkable story offers surprising insight in the relationship between native peoples and emigrants in the 1830s and 40s. The Whitmans trusted a Nez Perce woman to take their child more than 100 miles across wild country. There were no hotels or restaurants along the way, and no way to call for help if there was trouble. Movies and TV shows tend to portray "cowboys and Indians" stereotypes rather than the interdependent trusting relationships that were common in the early years of the American West.

CHAPTER
FOUR

Narcissa Whitman, wife of Marcus Whitman

IN NOVEMBER, 1847, Father took me again to Doctor Whitman's school. I was ten years old. In addition to the usual number of children in the school, Doctor Whitman had adopted a family of orphans named Sager.

The father and mother had been killed by the Indians on the plains. Doctor Whitman and his wife were wonderfully kind-hearted, and frequently took in both white and Indian children that were homeless. Their own little Alice, drowned in her infancy, was their only child.

When we arrived at the station everything seemed peaceful and quiet.

An overview of the Whitman Mission. On the right is the mission house where Eliza, Catherine Sager, and the other children had school. On the left is the grist mill, where Dr. Whitman ground the wheat into flour. The emigrant station was designed for the many Oregon Trail pioneers as they passed through on their way to the Willamette Valley.

An epidemic of measles was in progress among the Cayuses, and several white children were also suffering. Two or three children in Doctor Whitman's family were down and other families were experiencing the same inconvenience. The Doctor was busy taking care of his colony of invalids. Many of the Indians were dying in spite of his attentions, and, as the death rate increased, one could see that the Indians were growing restless. It was small wonder that they died, as they paid not the slightest attention to the orders of Doctor Whitman. He gave them medicine, of course, but as they had notions of their own about the cure for measles the medicine did them little good.

NOTES

EDITOR'S NOTE: Of course, we now know that there was little Whitman could do to help anyone with measles. Native people often died from the disease because they did not have the built-in immunity that people of European descent had. This sad scene played out often in the Americas—from the moment Columbus landed—killing millions.

Their method of ridding themselves of the bothersome disease was a hot steam bath, immediately followed by a plunge into an ice-cold stream. Their bathhouses were unique. They built a small round hut, placed hot stones in it, and poured water over the stones until a proper amount of steam was produced. Of course the plunge into the cold water after the sweat bath proved fatal to many of them, as they were in a weakened condition.

Father and Doctor Whitman, just a few days before school was to begin, went over to Umatilla, which was about thirty miles from the Whitman station, to visit the sick at that place. Doctor Whitman stayed two or three days, and was then compelled to hurry back to his home to take care of his own sick. Father stayed with the Umatilla Indians to preach to them and to aid the sick a while longer. It was this little fact that undoubtedly saved his life.

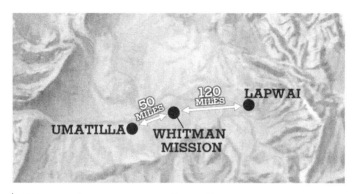

This map offers some perspective on Eliza's journey. It was 120 miles from her home in Lapwai to the Whitman Mission where she attended school. Umatilla, was 50 miles further on.

CHAPTER
FIVE

DOCTOR WHITMAN REACHED HOME on the Sabbath evening, and on the following morning, November 29, 1847, school began in one section of the log house that was used by Doctor and Mrs. Whitman and a number of whites in a sort of community fashion. We children were excited and happy as only youngsters can be on the first day of school.

SCHOOL

The "school" Eliza mentions is the back part of the Whitman's residence at the Whitman Mission.

Early in the morning, after we had gone upstairs to our work, Doctor and Mrs. Whitman and a Mrs. Osborn, who was rooming in another apartment of the house, were discussing the probability of an Indian outbreak. Mrs. Osborn told me of the conversation some time later. Doctor Whitman, she said, seemed worried over the outlook and talked freely of the rumors he had heard while at the Umatilla station. The attitude of the Indians there, he thought, was not as free as it was formerly, and the braves seemed to be sullen and evasive when he asked them questions as to their health.

He could not explain it in any way except that they were angry with him for some unknown reason.

"However," he said, "I don't think they will kill any one but Spalding and myself, if the worst comes to the worst. We are the leaders, and they will surely be content with us."

While they were talking, an Indian appeared at the door and asked for Doctor Whitman. The Doctor arose and led the Indian into a kitchen where he always talked with the Indians. There were several more in that room when he entered. He asked them quietly how the sick were getting along, and was talking composedly about the medicine the Indians said they wanted, when two of them slipped up behind him and struck him in the head with a tomahawk.

They gave the terrible war cry as they struck the foul blow that ended the life of one of God's truest servants.

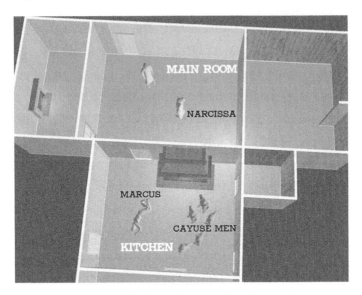

Marcus Whitman is killed in the kitchen. His wife is in the next room. The children are upstairs.

This was the signal for a general outbreak, and the Indians that were stationed at various points of the little mission began the general massacre. Men were shot down wherever they happened to be working at the time. No one was given a chance to defend himself. John Sager, the oldest of the orphans, was in the room with Doctor Whitman at the time of the killing. The Indians struck him down and cut his throat.

We children upstairs heard the firing and the awful yelling. We were pioneer children and knew quite well what it meant. Our teacher, a Mr. Sanders, went to the door; as soon as he opened it two or three Indians pounced on him and killed him in plain sight of the frightened group of children huddled in the corner. As they did not disturb us at the time we held a juvenile council of war, and we decided to hide in a sort of attic overhead. Some of the larger boys pulled some boards down and helped the smaller ones to get up.

NOTES

EDITOR'S NOTE: As a young girl, Eliza could not have known the exact factors that led to the killings—but she gives a tantalizing hint. She reports Whitman discussing the Indian's sickness just before Whitman was killed. Many historians cite a man named Joe Lewis, who tried to stir up the local tribes by claiming the Whitmans were purposely causing the illnesses. Lewis's motivation is not clear, but it's certainly true that frustration over disease was a major factor.

CHAPTER
SIX

THE INDIANS SOON RUSHED INTO THE schoolroom and called loudly for us to come down. We did not answer at first; but, realizing that it was worse than useless to "contrary" them, we at last answered and were pulled by rough hands from our hiding-place. There was not an outcry from any of the frightened tots. As I could talk with the savages I went up to one of them and asked him if he intended to kill us too. He gave me no answer, but his horrible look as he sneered at me was printed forever in my memory.

We were marched downstairs into the room where Doctor Whitman and Johnny Sager had been killed. Neither was quite dead when we got there, and we had to endure the horrible sight of their final death struggles. Johnny's younger brother Francis stepped up to the dying boy and spoke to him, but got no answer. Then Francis turned to me as pale as death and said quietly: "I will soon follow."

N O T E S

EDITOR'S NOTE: Eliza is ten years old when the attack takes place, but she is perhaps the most important eyewitness—because she can understand what the Cayuse men are saying. None of the other survivors have her command of the language—and Eliza is pressed into service as a translator.

We were huddled in one corner of the room, tense with the horror of the affair, waiting breathlessly for the command that would snuff out the lives of us all. And yet we did not whimper. Perhaps we were too frightened.

At last one of the leaders spoke up and said: "We won't kill any more of the women and children just now."

I wondered why he didn't finish the work quickly and not keep us in the torture of doubt, but afterward I realized that he wanted us for a screen to prevent the punishment that was sure to come to them when knowledge of their crime reached the outside.

Meantime Mrs. Whitman, when she heard the shots and the Indian yells, went to the door and watched in a dazed way the terrible carnage without. "Joe" Lewis, a halfbreed, whom the Whitmans had sheltered during the winter, stood near with a gun in his hand. Dumfounded at the thought of his treachery she asked him if he was taking any part in the outrage. For answer he pulled out a pistol and shot her. She fell to the floor seriously wounded. Andrew Rogers, who was spending the winter at the station, hurried to her aid and was shot in the arm. Mrs. Osborn, who had been talking with Doctor and Mrs. Whitman at the beginning of the tragedy, ran to her room and managed to hide herself and her four children under the floor.

CHAPTER
SEVEN

WHEN IT WAS NEARLY DARK, THE INDIANS held a consultation and decided to remove all the children and women that were still alive to an emigrant house, and to confine them there as prisoners. They ordered the children to march out. We were huddled together in a corner just outside the door of the building.

Mrs. Whitman, under Mr. Rogers's care, had sufficiently recovered from the effects of her wound to sit up. One of the older Indians called to her to come outside, as they wanted to take her to another house. She answered that she was afraid. The Indian, with a sarcastic smile on his face, told her that the trouble had been caused by some of the younger ones who had become angry. He said he was sorry for all the damage done, and that he wanted to make amends.

I knew by the way he looked and talked that he did not mean a word of it. It was part of a plan to end the life of the noble woman.

Mrs. Whitman was brought into the room where her dead husband lay, and when she saw the sight she fainted. The halfbreed Lewis and Mr. Rogers placed her on a lounge and carried her outside. Just as they reached the yard the halfbreed dropped his end of the lounge, and the Indians gave a yell as they fired at the man and the woman. Mr. Rogers fell to the ground dead. Mrs. Whitman was then shot again and beaten with a war club. We children, huddled in the corner within a few feet of them, saw the whole affair.

Francis Sager, who was standing between his sister Matilda and myself, was jerked from the crowd by a savage and shot down at our feet. Then I was certain that we would all be treated the same way. I put my apron over my head, as I didn't like to see the guns pointed at us. But the firing stopped then.

We were taken to a house across the yard and kept there as prisoners. During all that time not one of the children had even whimpered, much less screamed.

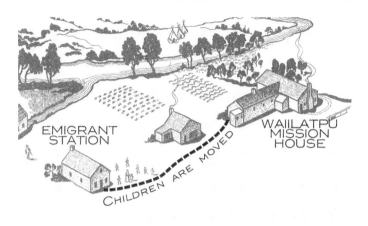

Eliza notes that the children were moved from the Mission House (right) to the Emigrant House.

It seems impossible that one could sleep after such a fearful experience, but we did. I slept soundly all that night, and when I awoke the next morning it was hard to realize that the terrible massacre had taken place. I tried to make myself believe that it was all a nightmare, and that I would find things as they were two days before. But with dead men scattered around the yard, with women around me whose faces were drawn and white, with Indian guards scattered here and there, it did not take long to convince myself that a tragedy had indeed taken place.

That morning the firing was kept up just enough to make it trying on the nerves. Mr. Kimble, who had been hiding all night, tried to get into the house. He was shot as he was climbing over a fence. We heard an Indian say: "See how I can make a white man tumble."

The little Kimble girl and I ran to a window, only to see her father roll off the fence to the ground. He had been killed by the savage who exulted in his marksmanship.

Mr. Canfield succeeded in eluding the guards and got into the house. His wife gave him a luncheon, and he prepared for a trip to my home to warn Mother. In a few days he reached Lapwai more dead than alive, and told the first news of the tragedy to Mother.

NOTES

EDITOR'S NOTE: After the initial fighting, Mr. Canfield hid in the loft of the Blacksmith shop (the small building between the Emigrant House and the Mission House). That night, he sneaked into the Emigrant House to speak to his wife, who was being held hostage there. She encouraged him to go for help, but Canfield wanted to stay and defend his family. They struck a deal: Canfield would hide away at a nearby hilltop until dawn. If the Indians seemed hostile, he would return and defend the women and children. But if there was no imminent visible danger, he would go to Lapwai for help. He did indeed go to Lapwai, and that's when Eliza's mother first learned what had happened.

A few days after the massacre, a priest came from Umatilla and took charge of the affairs at the Whitman station. Acting under his orders, the Indians buried the dead. The priest went through Doctor Whitman's property and found his medicine case. He gave it to the Indians and told them to bury it. His work done at the station, he and his halfbreed help prepared for the trip back to Umatilla.

I cannot explain it, but somehow I felt that I could trust the half breed. He looked honest, and afterward he justified my confidence in him. I told him to see my father without fail and tell him not to come to the station, as the Indians would certainly kill him. The half- breed promised. I had scarcely finished my instructions when an Indian came up and showed me a pistol.

"I am going with the priest, and when I meet your father I am going to kill him with this," he said, tapping the weapon.

NOTES

EDITOR'S NOTE: Eliza's sharp thinking may have saved her father's life. Henry Spalding was en route to the Whitman Mission, and would likely have been killed by the Cayuse—because Marcus Whitman and Henry Spalding were their primary targets. The priest (Father Brouillet) and his assistant did leave the site and warn Spalding—as Eliza has requested.

CHAPTER
EIGHT

I LIVED DAYS OF TORTURE UNTIL I HEARD that Father had escaped. On the way back they met him just starting for the Whitman station. The Indian who had told me he would kill Father had fired his pistol to light his pipe with the flint. He had not reloaded. As he thought Father would keep the trail he hurried back and hid around a ledge of rock.

NOTES

EDITOR'S NOTE: Eliza here skips a few details: After burying the dead, Father Brouillet left the Whitman Mission with two Indians. One was the "half-breed" Eliza trusted; the other was a Cayuse man intent on killing Eliza's father, Henry Spalding. Brouillet and the "half-breed" intercepted Spalding on the road as Spalding was approaching the Whitman Mission. Meanwhile the Cayuse man was laying in wait behind a rock.

Father asked the priest how the people at the

station were. The priest, after some hesitation, replied: "They are all dead." After giving this shocking answer he rode on.

NOTES

EDITOR'S NOTE: It's not clear why Brouillet would say "they're all dead," since about 50 women and children were still alive, and being held hostage.

The half breed stopped and told Father what I had said. There was a low fog down in the valley. The halfbreed advised Father to get into it and stay until darkness came on.

"When you come to the Walla Walla go either up or down stream, and don't go out on the opposite bank, in a straight line. This will throw them off the trail," the halfbreed advised. Father gave him two pack-horses to care for, and the half breed kindly insisted that Father take his luncheon of bread and meat.

NOTES

EDITOR'S NOTE:Again, this advice likely saved Spalding's life.

The waiting Indian back on the trail grew restless as Father did not appear, and he returned to the spot, taking up the trail. He lost it in the fog, but the next morning, with a party, he followed it to the

Walla Walla. They lost it there and gave up the chase.

Safely across the river Father urged his horse rapidly toward home. He was nearly captured by Indians who were searching the country near the present site of Spokane. He jumped from his horse and held the animal's nostrils to keep him from whinnying. The Indians saw the horse, and Father heard them decide that it was a stray one. He let the horse go and hid in a ditch while the Indians captured the animal. He lay hidden during the day and traveled at night. His boots hurt him so much that he threw them away and stumbled on barefoot. Miles of sharp stones and prickly-pear beds were ahead of him, but in spite of the torture he pushed on.

When he came to the Snake River near Alpowa he saw a large Nez Perce camp. He was starving and yet afraid to trust even his own Indians.

NOTES

EDITOR'S NOTE: The Nez Perce had nothing to do with the attack. The killing was done by a few Cayuse. While the two peoples did live near each other, they were separate tribes.

Crawling nearer he heard the evening service, and even heard the leader offer a prayer referring to the massacre and asking God to protect their "friend

Spalding." But as Father did not recognize the speaker's voice he was still afraid to show himself. He hid on a bluff of rocks and saw a band of Cayuses on the trail below. They were going to our mission to finish the work they had begun at the Whitman station. But the number of our Indians evidently discouraged the murderers when they came up, and they left without accomplishing their purpose.

NOTES

EDITOR'S NOTE: Once again, Spalding narrowly escapes the pursuing Cayuse.

CHAPTER
NINE

FATHER STARTED OUT AGAIN THAT NIGHT and came across an old Indian woman. He had been without food for six days, and he determined to risk everything. She told him that Mother had been taken ten miles away to the main camp, and that they thought "Father Spalding had been killed." He was so ragged and weak she did not recognize him.

NOTES

EDITOR'S NOTE: Spalding's journey was even more harrowing than Eliza describes. At one point, he lost his horse and had to walk about 90 miles. His shoes became so uncomfortable, he threw them away and walked barefoot on the frozen ground.

With the greatest relief he realized that he could make himself known. He staggered into the nearest tepee, and fell in a faint into the arms of old Luke, a faithful old soul, one of Father's best friends in the tribe. Luke was heartbroken when he saw Father's plight and he hurried to revive him. Indian women hastened to prepare nourishment for him, while others bathed his feet and sponged his face. The men were jubilant over the glad news that their "Father Spalding" was still alive, and they sent a runner to tell Mother.

Meanwhile, when Mr. Canfield reached Lapwai and told Mother of the massacre, she was, of course, nearly crazed with worry about Father and myself. To get more definite information about me she sent old Timothy and Eagle, two of our trusted Indians, to the Whitman station. They had one hundred and twenty miles to go, and reached the station nine days after the massacre, just as the Cayuses were killing two men who had been lying sick in the house, and who, it was feared, might get well and make an attempt to escape and rescue the prisoners. We captives could hear them groaning as the Indians beat them with war clubs. I shall never forget the look of disgust on Timothy's face as he came into the room where I was. "So that's the way the Cayuses kill!" he exclaimed; and then he sat down beside me, silently shaking his head as if in perplexing thought.

Timothy, a Nez Perce sent by Eliza's mother to

check on her. He was disgusted by the Cayuse's treatment of the people at the Whitman Mission.

How happy I was to see those two Indians! I thought I could go home with them, and when Timothy told me he couldn't take me with him, as the Cayuses had forbidden it, it seemed to me my heart was breaking. I cried for the first time during all the awful trouble. Timothy sympathized with me and wiped my eyes with my apron. "Eliza, don't cry," he said. "See Mother soon. We fix it." It was a terrible trial for me to watch the Indians leave without me, and yet I knew that they would be of great comfort to Mother when they told her I was safe.

NOTES

EDITOR'S NOTE: Timothy and Eagle could not take Eliza home because the Cayuse were holding the women and children hostage.

CHAPTER
TEN

WE WERE KEPT AT THE STATION FOR THREE weeks. We had plenty to eat, but the constant strain told on our nerves. There were, I think, fifty-nine women in the company of prisoners. As I understood the Indian language I had to act as interpreter between the white women and the savages. I became so weak that they had to lift me from bed in the mornings in case I had to get up for anything.

At last the glad tidings of delivery came. Our liberty had been bought by Peter Skeen Ogden, of the Hudson Bay Company, at Fort Vancouver. As soon as he heard of the massacre he filled boats with furs and provisions and started them up the Columbia, even though it was near the last of December and the weather was freezing cold. The Indians haggled for a while, trying to drive a sharp bargain, and then consented to release us for four hundred dollars, to be paid chiefly in blankets, ammunition and other things they wanted. So at last we were free.

Peter Ogden had to travel more than 250 miles to ransom the survivors. He was successful because he was highly respected by the native peoples.

As the Indians were still excited and might at any moment go back on their bargain and start another slaughter, we were hurried to Fort Walla Walla by ox-train at such a speed that on the thirty-mile trip two of the oxen dropped dead, and the rest were exhausted when we finally reached the fort.

It was decided that it would be safer to return to civilization, so Father and Mother were summoned to the fort. It was the beginning of winter, and they had one hundred and twenty miles to travel; but forty of the faithful Nez Perces acted as a bodyguard and brought the party safely through. How glad I was to see my father and mother once more! It seemed like a new life to be together again.

But we had little time to give way to our feelings. Almost immediately we had to start down the Columbia River. I was ill on the journey and remember little of it. We stayed in Oregon City until the following summer, and then settled on a claim in the Willamette Valley. I no longer had Matilda, Timothy and Eagle to care for me, and the playmates of my former days were gone forever.

IN THE autumn of 1849 five of the Indian murderers in the Whitman trouble were brought to Oregon City for trial. With a number of the women who had been captives, I was subpoenaed as a witness. It was trying on the nerves, and I think I was nearly as frightened in the courtroom as I was while held prisoner. The lawyers asked such questions about the massacre and the Indians looked so threatening that altogether it was a most unpleasant experience. The prisoners were convicted and sentenced to be hanged. They grew very much excited when told their doom, and said they wouldn't mind being shot, but to die by the rope was to die as a dog and not as a man.

In 1851 I lost my mother, and, being the oldest in the family, the cares of the household fell on my young shoulders. I accepted the duty cheerfully, as it meant a great deal to Father to have some one to help him. Three years later I got married. I was only sixteen years old. But we married much younger in those days than they do now. My husband was Andrew Jackson Warren, and, as he was a cattleman, we moved around a great deal during our married life.

While in the Walla Walla country Father and I

had a good visit with old Timothy-and a band of Nez Perces. The Indians came rushing up one day on their ponies when I was alone. I was frightened at first, as I thought maybe it was a band on the warpath; but my terror changed to joy when I finally saw who it was. Father was not at home that evening, and they waited impatiently for him until morning. What a grand time they did have talking over the old days at Lapwai!

AFTER A LAPSE OF SIXTY-TWO YEARS, in October, 1909, I revisited Lapwai. I was a widow then, and my father had also gone to his reward. A feeling of sacredness entered my heart as I reached the little village and went out to the spot where the old house had stood, and looked long and intently at the bluffs and hills where I had played as a girl. The Indians had made many improvements in their methods of living, and were paying gratifying atten-tion to better things. On the Sabbath I attended service in their little church, and talked to them through an interpreter, as I had forgotten the language during my years of absence from the tribe. Then they sang a song that Father taught them just before his death. After the meeting we had a regular love-feast. Every one of them shook hands with me, and some of the older men remarked: "This is Father Spalding's Eliza. I knew you when you were a little girl."

I am glad Father is buried right there among his Indians. As I looked at them neatly dressed and quite civilized I could not help comparing them with the Indians I knew when Father first started the work. It had been worth the sacrifice and the lives and the heartaches of it all.

Eliza (on the right) and her sister. This photo was taken around the time of her return to Lapwai in 1909. It's one of the few surviving images of Eliza.

ABOUT THE EDITOR

Michael Trinklein was a professor at Idaho State University for nearly 20 years. He wrote and produced *The Oregon Trail* documentary series for PBS. In addition, he has written for *The Wall Street Journal, The Boston Globe,* and *Time Magazine.* Mike's book *Lost States: True Stories of Texlahoma, Transylvania, and Other States That Never Made It* (Quirk Books) was a bestseller—*The New Yorker* called it, "a fascinating, funny book." Mike wrote all 20 hours of PBS' *Pioneers of Television* series, garnering 3 Emmy nominations. His graduate degree from The University of Iowa.

Made in the USA
Las Vegas, NV
11 July 2024